INSIDE THE
NBA FINALS

BY TODD KORTEMEIER

Published by The Child's World®
1980 Lookout Drive • Mankato, MN 56003-1705
800-599-READ • www.childsworld.com

Acknowledgments
The Child's World®: Mary Berendes, Publishing Director
Red Line Editorial: Design, editorial direction, and production
Photographs ©: Aaron M. Sprecher/AP Images, cover, 1; Icon Sports Media/Icon
Sportswire, 5; Bettmann/Corbis, 6; Mark J. Terrill/AP Images, 9; Jack Smith/AP Images,
10; ZumaPress/Icon Sportswire, 12; San Antonio Express-News/ZumaPress/Icon
Sportswire, 14; Kevin Reece/Icon Sportswire, 16; Icon Sportswire, 19; Tom DiPace/AP
Images, 20, 24; Lynee Sladky/AP Images, 23; Sue Ogrocki/AP Images, 26, 29

ISBN 9781634074360

LCCN 2015946278

Printed in the United States of America
Mankato, MN
December, 2015
PA02283

ABOUT THE AUTHOR

Todd Kortemeier is a writer and journalist from Minneapolis.
He is a graduate of the University of Minnesota's School of
Journalism & Mass Communication.

TABLE OF
CONTENTS

FAST FACTS

What is it? The National Basketball Association (NBA) Finals match the winners of the Western **Conference** and Eastern Conference to determine a champion. The **series** is best-of-seven games. That means the first team to win four games is the champion.

How do they qualify? Eight teams from each conference make the postseason. Teams must then win three playoff series to reach the finals.

What do they play for? NBA champions receive the Larry O'Brien Trophy. The NBA Championship Trophy was created in 1978. It was renamed after O'Brien in 1984. He was a NBA **commissioner**. The trophy is made of silver and gold. It depicts a life-sized basketball balancing on the edge of a hoop. The trophy weighs 16 pounds (7.26 kg).

When is it? Since 1984, the series has mostly been played in June. Before that it usually took place in May.

Where is it? The Finals are played on the home courts of the two teams. The team with the better regular-season record hosts Games 1, 2, and, if necessary, 5 and 7. The other team hosts Games 3, 4, and, if necessary, 6.

When was the first one? The first NBA Finals were held in April 1950. The Minneapolis Lakers defeated the Syracuse Nationals in six games. Before the NBA there was the Basketball Association of America (BAA). The first BAA Finals were held in 1947.

How many people go? NBA Finals games are usually sold out. The largest crowd in NBA Finals history was Game 5 in Detroit in 1988. That night, 41,732 fans came out to watch the Pistons battle the Los Angeles Lakers at the Silverdome.

How many people watch? Millions watch the NBA Finals each year. The 2015 series between the Golden State Warriors and the Cleveland Cavaliers averaged nearly 20 million viewers per game.

Chapter 1

A PLAYER'S PERSPECTIVE: THE BULLS' MICHAEL JORDAN

Michael Jordan sat in the locker room at the Great Western Forum. Game 5 of the 1991 NBA Finals had ended. Jordan and the Chicago Bulls had just won the title.

To his left was his wife. To his right was his father. In his arms was the Larry O'Brien Trophy. Jordan embraced it tightly. He had always believed this moment would come. But it had taken a long time to arrive.

"I'm still trying to let it sink in," Jordan said. "I've got seven years of it to sink in. It can't sink in in just a few hours, it's going to take a while. I don't know if I'm ever going to have this same feeling."[1]

◀ **Chicago Bulls guard Michael Jordan (in red) averaged just over 31 points per game during the 1991 NBA Finals.**

Jordan had already made his mark since entering the league in 1984. By the 1990–91 season, he already had led the NBA in scoring four times. He was the 1984–85 **Rookie** of the Year and the 1987–88 Most Valuable Player (MVP). But one thing had still eluded him: a championship.

The Bulls had been to the playoffs every year with Jordan. But they had not made the Finals. People had criticized Jordan. They thought he was a great scorer. But they said he did not do enough other things to help the Bulls win.

"You had all your media naysayers: 'Scoring champion can't win an NBA title. You're not as good as Magic Johnson. Not as good as Larry Bird. You're good, but you're not as good as those guys,'" Jordan said later. "I had to listen to this every day. That's why our first championship was a little sweeter."[2]

Jordan and the Bulls had swept the rival Detroit Pistons in the Eastern Conference Finals. Chicago had lost to them in that round the previous two years. Those losses had given the Bulls extra motivation.

The Finals were going to be tough. Chicago's opponents were Magic Johnson and the Los Angeles Lakers. The Lakers had been finalists many times. The Bulls had not.

Jordan celebrates as the Bulls clinch the 1991 NBA title over ▶ the Los Angeles Lakers.

"When we came out for Game 1, it was surreal," Bulls guard John Paxson said. "There were so many people on the court. It was like there was a fog in the building. It was almost madness."[3]

Maybe it was a little too overwhelming. The Bulls lost Game 1 93–91. But Jordan took over in Game 2. He made 15 of 18 shots and scored 33 points. Chicago won 107–86. The Bulls never looked back. They won all three games in Los Angeles to take the championship. Jordan was named Finals MVP.

After the last game, Jordan held the trophy and cried tears of joy.

"I want to enjoy this, it's such a great feeling," he said. "I've never been this emotional in public. When I came into this situation, we started from scratch. We started at the bottom and made it to the top. It's been a long, long seven years."[4]

Jordan and the Bulls won five more titles together. But on that night in 1991, Jordan was living in the moment.

"I'm not even thinking about any other championships right now," Jordan said. "I just want to enjoy this one for as long as I can."[5]

◀ Jordan was named NBA Finals Most Valuable Player each of the six times he and the Bulls won the title.

Chapter 2

A COACH'S PERSPECTIVE: THE SPURS' GREGG POPOVICH

Every day—that is how often San Antonio Spurs coach Gregg Popovich thought about Game 6 of the 2013 NBA Finals.

Three months had passed. He needed to prepare for a new season. But what had happened in Game 6 against the Miami Heat still haunted him.

"Without exception," he said. "I think about every play. I can see LeBron [James]'s first shot, and the rebound, and the second," Popovich said. "I've been . . . as sad as you can possibly be."[6]

The Spurs had been 5.2 seconds away from a fifth title. Security guards had started to prepare the court for a victory celebration. Heat fans had given up. They were streaming toward the exits. They missed a comeback for the ages.

◀ **San Antonio Spurs coach Gregg Popovich instructs his team during Game 6 of the 2013 NBA Finals.**

▲ **The Spurs bounced back from a disappointing end in 2013 to become champs in 2014.**

James started it with a 25-foot three pointer that cut the Spurs' lead to two. Spurs forward Kawhi Leonard was then **fouled**. He hit one of two free throws. With the Spurs up three, Popovich made a key move. He took center Tim Duncan out of the game. The Spurs center was the third-best playoff rebounder of all time. But he went to the bench.

So Duncan never got a chance to rebound James's next three-point attempt. Heat center Chris Bosh got it instead. He passed the ball to guard Ray Allen, who buried a three-pointer from the corner in the closing seconds. Tie game. The championship celebration would have to wait.

The Heat won in overtime. That forced a Game 7. No Heat fans left that one early, as Miami beat the Spurs to win the title.

As tough as Game 6 was, Popovich had no regrets about not playing Duncan.

"No," he said, when asked if he would do things differently. "You do what you do to win the game."[7]

Popovich continued to think about the loss every day. But he did not just dwell on it. He and the Spurs got to work.

"We went through every single play of Game 6 and Game 7," he said. "We made them sit through it. It's on us to see what we can do to get back into that same position. Can we or can't we?"[8]

They did. They faced a familiar foe in the 2014 Finals. It was the Heat. This time, the Spurs won the series 4–1.

"You have no reason not to be thankful every day that you have the opportunity to come back from a defeat," Popovich said. "Some people never even have the opportunity. So it's the measure of what you're worth, what you're made of."[9]

Chapter 3

THE CHEERLEADERS' PERSPECTIVE: LAKER GIRLS

Being a Los Angeles Lakers cheerleader is tough. They have to be at the arena hours before games start, just like players. They stretch, practice, and prepare for that night's game.

The Laker Girls stepped it up for the 2004 NBA Finals. They added another dance routine, increasing their total to seven. They also added two more dancers, bringing the squad to 18. A Laker Girl named Shannon had been on the squad for three seasons. She and the other girls knew how intense the Finals were.

"The atmosphere is completely different," Shannon said. "There are cameras everywhere, and everyone's got this nervous energy, wherever you go."[10]

The Laker Girls were founded in 1979. Team owner Jerry Buss wanted more excitement at games. They were the NBA's first

◄ **The Laker Girls have been entertaining fans in Los Angeles since 1979.**

cheerleading squad. Today, every team has its own cheerleaders. The Laker Girls are some of the best.

The squad performed between 17 and 25 different routines each season. They had at least three costume changes per game. But the Laker Girls were more than just dancers. They were also huge fans.

"We are into every moment of the game," Shannon said during the 2004 playoffs. "We are watching the plays, yelling at the refs, doing all that stuff—we're fans, too."[11]

Lakers fans everywhere certainly enjoyed the team's 2003–04 playoff run. The 2002–03 season had been a disappointment. The Lakers did not make it out of the second round of the playoffs. But they made the Finals the next season.

"Last year, I think with every game we were nervous, like come on guys, come on, we can do this, we can do this," Shannon said. "That last game last year, I know all of us were very disappointed along with the team. But this year everyone believes."[12]

That special NBA Finals energy Shannon talked about affected everyone. The Laker Girls and the players could feel it. So could the fans.

"[The fans] are more inclined to be cheering and stay in their seats and stay 'til the end of the game," Shannon said. "I think

▲ **Los Angeles won the NBA title in the Laker Girls' first season.**

everyone's really excited and really, really pulling for the Lakers to go all the way."[13]

The team spirit was there. But unfortunately it was not enough. Los Angeles lost to the Detroit Pistons 4–1 in the NBA Finals.

Chapter 4

AN OWNER'S PERSPECTIVE: THE MAVERICKS' MARK CUBAN

It was 2006. The Dallas Mavericks were in the NBA Finals against the Miami Heat. Mavericks owner Mark Cuban was not happy during Game 5. His team was on its way to losing its third game in a row. Cuban was angry with the **referees**. He believed they were officiating the game unfairly.

Cuban was upset at the number of fouls called against Dallas. He went down onto the court after the loss. He argued with the referees face-to-face. Then, he gave a profanity-filled rant when speaking with reporters. His actions resulted in a $250,000 **fine** from the NBA.

"I think the pressure of his first Finals may be getting to him," NBA Commissioner David Stern said.[14]

◀ **Dallas Mavericks owner Mark Cuban (middle) celebrates with two of his players during Game 6 of the 2011 NBA Finals.**

Cuban had bought the Mavericks in 2000. He was a fan and season-ticket holder before becoming an owner. Since taking over, he had been fined more than $1 million for many violations.

Flash forward to 2011. The Mavericks were again in the Finals. And again they were playing the Heat. But one thing was different. Cuban kept quiet. He let his team's play do the talking.

"[Cuban] was great about it," Mavericks coach Rick Carlisle said. "He understood and he knew it was the right thing. . . . He was extremely disciplined during this run and it helped us."[15]

"It didn't make any sense to say anything," Cuban said. "The quieter I got, the more we won."[16]

Even when the Heat went up 2–1 in the series, Cuban said nothing. He never came down to the court. He never joined in team timeouts. He never yelled at the referees. He just watched nervously with all the fans. The Mavericks won three games in a row. In the deciding Game 6, Dallas closed in on the championship. But Cuban did not want to think too far ahead.

"I just remember the last time we were in Miami [in 2006] in that Game 3 where we're up and I'm thinking we've got a chance to **sweep**," Cuban later said.[17]

For better or worse, Cuban has been one of the most vocal ▶ owners in the NBA since taking over the Mavericks in 2000.

But in the final seconds, it was clear the Mavericks were going to win. Cuban came down from his seat and joined his players. After the buzzer sounded, Cuban became his normal, vocal self.

"Did anybody inform you guys we're the world champions?!" Cuban shouted as he walked into the post-game press conference.[18]

He then spoke about his players. He thanked them for laying it all on the line to win the title. He praised their heart and determination. It was not easy, but they had achieved their ultimate goal together.

"My biggest fear is that I can't remember every little part of it, every emotion, every feeling that I went through as the clock was winding down," Cuban said. "So that's my biggest hope and fear that I'll be able to feel this forever."[19]

◀ **In 2011, Dallas forward Dirk Nowitzki (left) and the Mavericks avenged their 2006 NBA Finals loss.**

Chapter 5

THE FANS' PERSPECTIVE: THUNDER FANS

The sports scene in the state of Oklahoma was pretty limited. The University of Oklahoma had a popular and successful football program. And Oklahoma State University had a strong wrestling team. But the **professional** sports landscape was bare.

That was until 2005. Hurricane Katrina damaged the arena of the New Orleans Hornets. They needed a new home. So they moved to Oklahoma City for two years. The experiment was successful. Oklahoma City showed it was worthy of having its own NBA team.

In 2008, the Seattle SuperSonics moved. They became the Oklahoma City Thunder. The fans were excited to get a team. But it was not a very good one. The first Thunder team started its debut season 3–29 and finished 23–59.

◄ **Fans in Oklahoma City have shown their support for the Thunder since the team's arrival in 2008.**

But things had turned around by 2012. Forward Kevin Durant had become one of the NBA's best players. He and guards Russell Westbrook and James Harden formed a "Big Three." They rolled all the way to the Finals and met the Miami Heat. Oklahoma City had become a basketball town.

"This is the biggest thing we've had here," Thunder fan Tony Wright said. "This is it."[20]

The success pained Seattle fans. Their Sonics had been taken away. Now the team was playing for a title in another city.

"The first thing you do is to try not to be a hater," Slick Watts, a former Sonics player, said. "But as a fan, you feel they should be here."[21]

The Thunder had home-court advantage for the Finals. That was valuable. Oklahoma City had a noisy home crowd. Many of the 18,000 fans wore blue Thunder T-shirts. In the Western Conference Finals, 7,000 more people had showed up just to watch outside the arena on big screens.

"Our players, they love playing here. They know every night that we're going to have the best crowd in the game," Thunder coach Scott Brooks said. "They're going to come out and they're going to cheer you on."[22]

The fans were out in force for Game 1. Seemingly everything in Oklahoma City was painted the team's blue and orange colors.

▲ **Superstars Kevin Durant (left) and Russell Westbrook greet thousands of fans at the airport after the 2012 NBA Finals.**

That even included some fans' hair. The crowd arrived early and cheered throughout the game. At the end, when the Thunder clinched the win, the crowd chanted "MVP! MVP!"[23] for their best player. Durant had 36 points, 17 of them coming in the fourth quarter.

But things took a turn for the worse. The Thunder dropped four straight games to lose the series. Still, the city showed its support. When the Thunder got home from Miami, more than 4,000 fans were waiting at the airport. A few of the players spoke, including Durant.

"Last night was one of the toughest times we've ever had as a group," he said. "But coming back home we knew we'd see you guys, and we really appreciate it."[24]

GLOSSARY

commissioner (kuh-MISH-uh-ner): The commissioner is the person in charge of the NBA. Larry O'Brien was an NBA commissioner.

conference (KON-frence): A conference is a group of teams. The NBA is divided into the Eastern Conference and Western Conference.

fine (fine): A fine is a financial penalty for a rule violation. Dallas Mavericks owner Mark Cuban got a fine for going onto the court to argue with officials.

fouled (fould): Players are fouled when opponents do something against the rules to try to stop them from making a play. Dallas Mavericks owner Mark Cuban was upset that officials thought his team fouled the Miami Heat so often during the 2006 NBA Finals.

professional (pruh-FESH-uh-nul): A professional sport is one in which athletes are paid to play. Oklahoma did not have any major permanent professional teams before the Thunder arrived in 2008.

referees (REFF-urr-ees): Referees enforce the rules on the court during a game. The referees called many fouls against the Dallas Mavericks during the 2006 NBA Finals.

rookie (ROOK-ee): A rookie is a first-year player. Michael Jordan was named Rookie of the Year for the 1984–85 season.

series (SEER-ees): A series is a number of games played in a single playoff round. The NBA Finals are a best-of-seven series.

sweep (sweep): A sweep is when a team wins a series without losing a game. The Dallas Mavericks had a chance to sweep the Miami Heat in 2006.

SOURCE NOTES

1. "Bulls Finally Get That Championship Feeling." *NBA.com*. NBA Media Ventures. n.d. Web. 20 May 2015.

2-3. Bryan Smith. "Inside the Start of the Chicago Bulls' Championship Run." *Chicago Magazine*. Chicago Tribune Media Group. 11 Apr. 2011. Web. 20 May 2015.

4-5. "Bulls Finally Get That Championship Feeling." n.d.

6. Ben Golliver. "Gregg Popovich Still Thinks About Game 6 'Every Day,' but Spurs Are Built to Bounce Back." *Sports Illustrated*. Time Inc. 24 Sep. 2013. Web. 3 Jun. 2015.

7. Buck Harvey. "At Last, Summer Ending for Popovich." *San Antonio Express-News*. Hearst Communications Inc. 19 Sep. 2013. Web. 3 Jun. 2015.

8-9. J. A. Adande. "Spurs' Fortitude Fueled Title Run." *ESPN*. The Walt Disney Company. 20 Nov. 2014. Web. 3 Jun. 2015.

10-13. Jennifer Nelson. "The Other View from the Court: A Laker Girl's Perspective." *NBA.com*. NBA Media Ventures. 8 Jun. 2004. Web. 3 Jun. 2015.

14. David DuPree. "NBA Fines Cuban $250,000 for Behavior After Game 5." *USA Today*. Gannett Company. 21 Jun. 2006. Web. 4 Jun. 2015.

15-16. "Mark Cuban Defers Praise After Win." *ESPN*. The Walt Disney Company. 13 Jun. 2011. Web. 4 Jun. 2015.

17. Jeff Caplan. "Mark Cuban Let his Team Make Noise." *ESPN*. The Walt Disney Company. 14 Jun. 2011. Web. 4 Jun. 2015.

18-19. "Mark Cuban Defers Praise After Win." 13 Jun. 2011.

20. "Thunderstruck: OKC Fans Go Crazy for NBA." *CBS DFW*. CBS Local Media. 11 Jun. 2012. Web. 4 Jun. 2015.

21. John Hickey. "Seattle Mourns Loss of Possible NBA Champion Thunder." *USA Today*. Gannett Company. 11 Jun. 2012. Web. 4 Jun. 2015.

22. "Thunderstruck: OKC Fans Go Crazy for NBA." 11 Jun. 2012.

23. "Kevin Durant, Thunder, Pull Away from Heat, Win Game 1." *ESPN*. The Walt Disney Company. 14 Jun. 2012. Web. 4 Jun. 2015.

24. "Thousands of Fans Greet Thunder After Finals Loss." *NBA.com*. NBA Media Ventures. 22 Jun. 2012. Web. 4 Jun. 2015.

TO LEARN MORE

Books

De Medeiros, Michael. *The NBA*. New York: AV2 by Weigl, 2013.

Editors of Sports Illustrated. *Basketball's Greatest*. New York: Time Home Entertainment, 2014.

Editors of Sports Illustrated Kids. *Sports Illustrated Kids Big Book of Who Basketball*. New York: Time Home Entertainment, 2015.

Web Sites

Visit our Web site for links about the NBA Finals: childsworld.com/links

Note to Parents, Teachers, and Librarians: We routinely verify our Web links to make sure they are safe and active sites. So encourage your readers to check them out!

INDEX